THE
HIGH WEALD
IN OLD PHOTOGRAPHS

This book is dedicated to the memory of the late C.H. 'Charlie' Bocking (above) who collected, chronicled and collated the history of Wadhurst and its locality for most of his life; and also to Ruth Collingridge (pictured on p. 158) who performed an equally dedicated service for Ticehurst. The majority of the photos of Wadhurst and Ticehurst which follow are taken respectively from their voluminous collections.

THE
HIGH WEALD
IN OLD PHOTOGRAPHS

COMPILED BY

BRIAN HARWOOD

To Alec,

With Compliments

ALAN SUTTON

Alan Sutton Publishing Limited
Phoenix Mill · Far Thrupp · Stroud · Gloucestershire

First Published 1990

British Library Cataloguing in Publication Data

The High Weald in old photographs.
1. East Sussex. (District) Wealden, history
I. Harwood, Brian *1936–*
942.251

ISBN 0-86299-704-6

Front Cover Illustration:
MISS E.G. COUCHMAN AND MRS C. BOORMAN in the hop gardens of Yew Tree Farm, Wadhurst.

Typeset in 9/10 Korinna.
Typesetting and origination by
Alan Sutton Publishing Limited.
Printed in Great Britain by
The Guernsey Press Co. Ltd
Guernsey, Channel Islands

INTRODUCTION

The Ice Age glaciation of some two million years ago covered the land mass that would one day re-emerge as the British Isles only down as far as the Severn-Thames line; southwards from here extended a vast frozen tundra from which protruded a low crest of snow-capped hills. The ice retreated, the tundra warmed and dried, then, relieved from the pressure of its massive frozen shroud, the land rose above the surrounding water level. Great forests grew across the steaming, damp soils of the south, mostly of oak and beech, for these thrived and proliferated like weeds in an alluvium supported upon an impermeable bed of clay from 200 to 800 ft thick. Some of those original trees survive today, not as wood, but in fossil stone just off the beaches of Cliff End and Pett, as many an unwary swimmer will attest. For the great forest ran south across the Channel deep into France and Germany where larger remnants survive today than do here at its northern extremity. We have the New Forest, the Forest of Dean and Savernake Forest to the west to remind us how most of Sussex once looked, but only the Sussex Weald – our primeval snow-capped crest of hills – survives, and more through geological chance than by man's initiative.

The Weald, or woods, was for millenia a virtually impenetrable jungle. Settlers migrating northwards from the continent found precarious livings among the cathedral-like naves of massive oaks, with their huge unchecked canopies shutting out light for much of the year. Life in the lower forest levels was rendered worse by the continual flooding as rising rivers meandered far and wide seeking a drain through the clay beds. Thus most permanent settlements became established at the top, the High Weald, where the drier land could be worked to some advantage. Up here the water became an ally for, racing down narrow clefts, or ghylls, its force was harnessed to drive simple machinery for pottery, wood-turning, and tool-making.

Small settlements in the forest became larger, but not much, for every locality was of necessity self-sufficient and self-contained because of the difficulties of communication over any distance. Most journeys undertaken on the ill-drained terrain were of short duration, and so communities were generally spaced about four miles from each other – near enough to be in touch, far enough not to be continually disturbed. This gave rise to the strange Sussex phenomenon of short, apparently rambling trackways which still criss-cross the Weald today and which are not suitable for the motorist. But, in their day, these tracks, hardly roads, linked centres of forestry and, later, iron production with distribution points on the rivers Rother, Teise and Medway which were then navigable to the foot of the Wealden slopes.

Secure in their sprinkled settlements the indigenous High Wealdsmen survived the depredations of, successively, the Romans, Saxons, and Normans. Each invader took something from the forests, but gave nothing back. Nevertheless the basic lifestyle of the locals continued much as before; they merely learned to trade their woodland expertise in new tongues and coin, generally at a profit. But then things started to deteriorate as the basic material, the forest, began to disappear in totality. Wood for thousands of ships and countless tons of charcoal depleted the Weald's natural resource so dramatically that official restrictions on tree-felling were strictly administered. The timely message was heeded and subsequent generations of wood-workers, down to today, are grateful for the still quite extensive Wealden forest handed down to their keeping. And the men of the present have ensured the woods of the future by forming representative societies such as the Sussex Men of the Trees, and the Society of Sussex Downsmen, bodies whose advice is seriously heeded by the county councils.

The traditional theme of personal self-sufficiency, so necessary in the isolated High Weald communities, is borne out in the many diverse trades held by individuals at the same time. As some of these photographs reveal, this characteristic has persisted until quite recent times. Similarly, an important factor in this remoteness of settlement was the social protectiveness of each community for its members. This was perhaps most notably expressed in the era of the Sussex smuggler as, in their home environment of agreed anonymity and averted eyes, they freely secreted contraband in ponds and copses. Rudyard Kipling's 'Five-and-twenty ponies trotting through the dark' will be met with in real life through some of the following photographs. But, for any stranger pausing for refreshment at some of the inns depicted, not much might appear to have changed even today as they will encounter gentlemen of mahogany sunburn, gold ear ornaments, lavish tattoos, with hair tied back, apparently deep in conspiratorial discussion. In fairness, though, it has to be said that lawlessness has not always had a strong hold here, for each village has its own distinctive church, most very ancient, all appealing. Additionally, finding a foothold at isolated road junctions and in woodland clearings were (and still are) many chapels of various denominations.

The High Weald photographic survey that follows depicts many of the social and geographic aspects described above in the various localities which are found along the crest and flanks of the Wealden ridge. Travelling west to east these are Frant, Bells Yew Green, Wadhurst, Cousley Wood, Ticehurst, Flimwell, and Etchingham, plus many isolated communities in the countryside between the villages.

Much has not survived on record however. We can best gauge the extent of change through the medium of photographs — we look at then and now. But each year, each day, many hundreds of these photographs, unique irreplaceable records, get discarded. So, in respect of these Wealden communities at least, may the author urge the reader, when contemplating a 'clear out', to pause a moment and consider whether the photo destined for the dustbin might not be a unique record for future generations. If it is, please keep it in, or take it to, a place of safety.

See you the ferny ride that steals
Into the oak-woods far?
O that was whence they hewed the keels
That rolled to Trafalgar.

And mark you where the ivy clings
To Bayham's mouldering walls?
O there we cast the stout railings
That stand around St Paul's.

See you the dimpled track that runs
All hollow through the wheat?
O that was where they hauled the guns
That smote King Philip's fleet.

(Out of the Weald, the secret Weald,
Men sent in ancient years
The horse-shoes red at Flodden Field,
The arrows at Poitiers!)

See you our little mill that clacks,
So busy by the brook?
She has ground her corn and paid her tax
Ever since Domesday Book.

See you our stilly woods of oak,
And the dread ditch beside?
O that was where the Saxons broke
On the day that Harold died.

(Puck of Pook's Hill — Rudyard Kipling)

VIEW OF ETCHINGHAM, FROM THE OLD ROAD HURST GREEN SUSSEX.

A CHARACTERISTIC HIGH WEALD VIEW.

AN EARLY VIEW of Etchingham post office and stores with, to the right, the old Etchingham Arms which burnt down around 1912.

A VIEW OF FLIMWELL painted in 1905 by W.C. Elliott.

WADHURST HIGH STREET at the turn of the century. On the right is Couchman's chemists and veterinary shop. The way the road level has progressively risen is seen by the drop to the shops on the left. It was not given a permanent tarmac surface until between the wars; before then it consisted of a base of Kentish rag, with cut stone rolled down on top. Periodically it was all dug up, relaid and rolled to remove the uneven parts.

THE ETCHINGHAM POST OFFICE SHOP near the church, in the 1920s. The proprietor, H.F. Tester, is standing to the left, with the previous postmaster, Mr Cox, between the white-clad boys. These are the Waters brothers, and the postman is Tom Roff.

COOPER'S STORES IN TICEHURST, depicted around 1867. At this time it was known as Pettit & Sanders, which name was retained until 1876 when it changed to Cooper's, which has persisted until today. One of the nearby properties was, in the 1860s, the Unicorn public house. Its landlord, William Stapely, was a former member of the infamous Hawkhurst Gang of smugglers – the southern counties' mafia of its day. Over the pub fireplace Mr Stapely kept his spurs, stirrup irons and bit; he was, according to C.J. Newington speaking in 1895, '... a quiet, reserved man and did not throw much light on his past history.'

COOPER'S STORES, C. 1860. Note the mounting-block and tethering rails. The earliest known owner is James Hine of 1767, but some Pashley papers of 1518 say '... John Eagles holdeth a shop at the Church Gate, Ticehurst'. If this preceded Cooper's, or was the house seen centre picture, is unknown. The Victoria County History (1937) dated parts of the stores fabric as c. 1600.

THE BRECKNOCK ARMS AND STORES at Bells Yew Green still remain important social centres of village life, as they have done for well over a century. The present pub was preceded by the Turk's Head, which brewed its own ale, but when the Brecknock Arms was built in the late 1800s, the brewery was re-established by the Ware family half a mile away up the Frant road (see p.125).

THIS VIEW OF WADHURST HIGH STREET, looking like a film set waiting for 'action' to be called, dates from around the 1860s. The ancient half-timbered building to the left is Gobles stores today; halfway along on the left is Washwell Lane (at that time known as Sheepwash Lane); in the distance, with ladders against it, is the Queen's Head Inn.

TICEHURST VILLAGE WELL after its completion in 1888. The first step towards building the well came in 1885 with a fund-raising bazaar, promoted principally by the Newington and Eden families. In Jubilee year, 1897, the original glass roof was replaced by a tiled one, and a new double-action pump installed. The timbers supporting the roof were said to have come from the old Ticehurst windmill. The large building in the background is Mr Farley's forge.

CHURCH STREET, TICEHURST, in the 1880s.

THIS PHOTO, dating from 1937, shows Roy Willard, Eric Crane, and Lionel Dengate outside the car repair shop of Covell & Foord, Etchingham. The building was originally (in the 1850s) the Black Eagle pub for the workers building the Hastings railway. It was sited on the estate of Haremere, and Thomas Russell, who owned the estate from 1875 to 1920, would not have a pub on his land, so it was renamed the Temperance Hotel. Today, Flint Timber (Bromley) Ltd occupies the site.

THE CASTLE CORNER CROSSROADS to Sparrows Green and Durgates, seen around 1911. The firm of H.J. Austen & Sons originally operated from Marling Place. After Frank Austen died, in 1909, the offices were moved to the premises shown in 1910. They moved down to Wadhurst High Street in 1913. The carrier's van shown is that of James Styles.

ROAD RESURFACING with rolled ragstone chippings at Gloucester Place, Sparrows Green, c. 1911. Roadman Edward Blackman is on the extreme right. Sussex roads have always had a bad press, as exemplified by a Lord Chancellor's comment in 1690: 'Sussex ways are bad and ruinous beyond imagination – 'tis a melancholy consideration that men will inhabit such a heap of dirt for a poor livelihood. The county is a sink!'

EDWARD BLACKMAN, Wadhurst roadman, pictured around 1912.

ST MARY'S LANE, TICEHURST, viewed from the church, probably in the 1880s. The old weather-boarded house at the extreme left used to have a large oak chest with a false bottom that smugglers could hide their wares in. Often the house and chest were searched and nothing found, when the false bottom would be full of lace. Contraband spirit kegs used to be hidden in the pond at the bottom right of the picture. These facts were related to Ticehurst historian Julia O'Dell by Thomas Skinner who died in 1901 aged 89. Mr Skinner worked at Pashley all his life from the age of ten and, walking there and back each day, covered a total distance estimated to be the equivalent of three times round the earth. His father and grandfather also worked there as servants so giving the Wetherall family at Pashley, between them all, some two centuries of service. The old smugglers' house survived until the 1970s.

THE ERIDGE HUNT AT THE GREYHOUND, c. 1890, for centuries the popular 'farmers' inn' of Wadhurst. The entrance to the market used to be along the path to the right of the inn. For most of the Victorian years, from 1856 to 1898, the landlord was Jacob Pitt, a renowned Wadhurst tradesman and great all-round cricketer. By a strange coincidence Maurice Tate, the Sussex and England all-rounder, was also the licensee of the Greyhound in the mid-1950s. He died in an upstairs room there and now rests in the nearby churchyard, barely a wicket's length from Jacob Pitt. The open space in front of the Greyhound was always a focal point for Wadhurst public gatherings, while to the rear of the inn used to be an extensive orchard leading to a hop garden. The barn in the background (recently demolished) had a timber 'queen strut' roof, denoting a venerable antiquity; at the time of the photo it was being used as a slaughterhouse.

INGLES FARMHOUSE, WADHURST, around 1934.

WADHURST STATION in 1933 showing, to the left, the original Railway Hotel.

AN AERIAL VIEW OF TICEHURST in 1952.

THIS VERY RARE VIEW OF WADHURST appeared in *Sussex in the Twentieth Century*, published in 1910 by W.T. Pike & Co., Brighton. The whereabouts of the original and the identity of the engraver remain, at present, unknown. Several copies were made by the late J.H. Chapman of Pell House which he distributed to various local friends. Identification of the buildings is uncertain, but extreme right is the old house called Clavers, while the half-timbered house to the left may be the original Old Queen's Head. The grandson of Jabez Smith, Mr W.G. Boyes, said his grandfather knew the Old Queen's Head to be some 600 years old (see pp. 14 & 59).

Queen's Head Hotel, Wadhurst.

THE QUEEN'S HEAD HOTEL as known to many generations of Wadhurst folk. Of indeterminate age, probably sixteenth-century, it was a focal point of village life until 1956 when it was destroyed by a crashing aircraft. The site remained derelict for some three years until the present shopping façade was built. This Queen's Head is not to be confused with the Old Queen's Head, an even more ancient inn that occupied property on the site of the existing Gobles shop.

WADHURST HIGH STREET around 1927.

WADHURST HIGH STREET from the same viewpoint some thirty years later immediately after being wrecked by a crashing jet aircraft.

THE CENTRE OF ONE SIDE of Wadhurst High Street was obliterated in the mid-afternoon of Friday 20 January 1956 by an RAF plane crash. The Queen's Head Hotel and the adjoining International Stores were wrecked, together with cottages in Washwell Lane where Thomas Stemp, 74, and Emily Reed, 57, his housekeeper, died. The aircrew, also killed, were FO Leonard Stoates, a Wadhurst man, and navigator Alastair Patterson from Ayrshire. The inquest decided that the pilot lost control by flying at too low an altitude, and that the plane was far off course for its training exercise.

THE TICEHURST LOWER TOLLGATE at Singehurst. Standing extreme left is Amos French, a postman for forty years, who opened the little general stores round the corner in Flimwell Road which continues to the present day. Above the front door of the cottage can be seen the tollboard listing the charges for each type of transport wishing to use the road. An example of such a tollboard can be seen at the Weald & Downland Museum, Singleton.

EXAMPLES OF ORIGINAL TICEHURST TOLL TICKETS, unfortunately undated. Both upper and lower toll cottages survive to the present day, not very much changed in external appearance. The Turnpike Trust of 1767, covering the Mayfield to Wadhurst road had, eventually, some nineteen separate toll gates along its length.

THE TICEHURST UPPER TOLLGATE at Cross Lane junction. The Wadhurst to Ticehurst road was first given toll status on its upgrading in 1767.

TICEHURST VILLAGE SQUARE pictured around 1907. On the extreme left is the wall to Mr Farley's forge. The Duke of York Hotel traces its ancestry back to c. 1602, commemorating maybe Charles Stuart, 7th Duke of York, 1605–16.

THE VIEW INTO TICEHURST around 1860.

THE SAME VIEW around 1938. A predecessor of the Chequers is mentioned in 1752 when landlord Isaac Tuppenny 'at the sign of the Exchequer' sold a bottle of rum for use of the vicar, Ossory Medlicott. The latter was well-known for his liking for payments in kind.

THIS REMOTE DWELLING down in Snape Wood, Wadhurst, was once called The Locomotive, being then an inn for the refreshment of the navvies working on the nearby railway in the 1850s. After they moved on and took their trade down the line, the inn was renamed The Miner's Arms in commemoration of the surrounding iron mine workings. It is today a private house. It is pictured in the early 1920s when it had also acquired the local nicknames of The Shant, or The Stream. It was converted to a private residence in 1955.

THE DECORATED ARCHES across the Wadhurst road in Ticehurst are for the wedding of Dr Samuel Newington's daughter, Catherine, to the Revd A.G.P. Humfrey of Thorpe Mandeville. The date is 22 August 1877. The premises at the extreme left are identified as 'Mr & Mrs Wright's Sweet Shop'. The Ticehurst arches were erected for all prominent weddings and public celebrations. Note the old chap to the left dressed in his best smock for the occasion.

THE OLD ETCHINGHAM ARMS or, more correctly, de Echyngham Arms, pictured post-1912 at around which time its predecessor on the site had burnt down.

FLIMWELL HIGH STREET around 1872, looking towards Hawkhurst. One of the small boys on the left is identified as Will Pankhurst.

THE A21 CROSSROADS AT FLIMWELL, around 1930. The event depicted is uncertain, though the rear of the Hare and Hounds seems to be acting as a meeting place – possibly for a sale?

WADHURST UPPER HIGH STREET in the mid-1930s. (Compare with p. 10.)

CHURCH STREET, TICEHURST, in the mid-1800s. In the house to the extreme right several members of the Startin family were born and brought up. A notable member was Alexander Charles, proprietor of the family building business, originally established in 1784.

THE 'DOWN' PLATFORM AT WADHURST STATION, C. 1907, typifying the spirit of the old SE & CR ('Slow, Easy and Comfortable') era. Seated centre is station master J. Martin, who retired in 1914 after eighteen years service. The dense woodland through which the line passes south of Wadhurst caused problems in steam days when cinders set fire to the lineside trees. Today the forest perennially gets its own back on the modern electric trains by liberally shedding 'leaves on the line'.

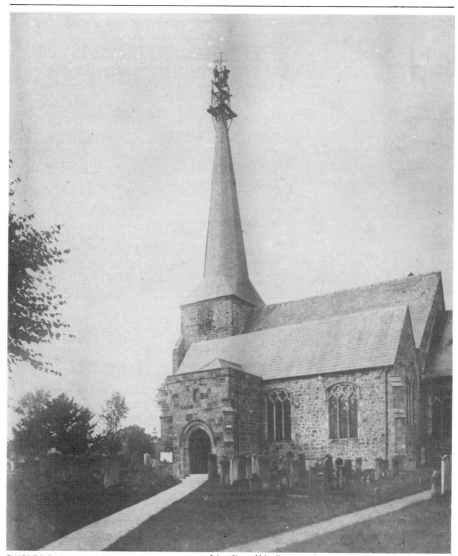

CHARLES BASSETT, WITH NEPHEW JOHN, re-shingling Wadhurst church in September 1897.
Although hampered by a steel caliper and special boot for a crippled leg, Charles spent
most of his working life aloft steeples, until his death in 1923 aged 67. The re-shingling
business was carried on by Thomas Bassett who, before his death in 1963 aged 77, had
worked on over 200 churches in the home counties. His original workshop stood from 1890
on the old Pritchards Garage site, where he was a wheelwright and coachbuilder,
specializing in the traditional Sussex Wagon. Some five years after this photograph was
taken John (sometimes called Jack) left shingling to set up the widely-known Durgates
Forge in 1902, using as capital 32 sovereigns earned as a shingler. He died in 1974 aged
92. One of his clearest memories of the time of this photograph was that he could run from
Durgates to the top of the Wadhurst church spire scaffolding in ten minutes.

NOTICE.

Conviction for disturbing a Congregation.

At the Petty Sessions holden at **Hurstgreen**, on **Friday 10th. May, 1861,** *Frank Chapman*, of **Ticehurst, Labourer, aged about 18 years, was convicted before Her Majesty's Justices of the Peace, for laughing and otherwise disturbing the Congregation on several occasions during Divine Service, at the Parish Church of Ticehurst, and fined in the sum of 5s. and 16s. costs, and in default of payment, to be imprisoned for 30 days in the County Gaol at Lewes.**

Ticehurst, May 31st. 1861.

G. F. Balcombe, Printer, Ticehurst.

THE VICTORIANS took their worship seriously!

CLERGY AND CHOIR OF WADHURST PARISH CHURCH around 1908. Clergy: Revd L. Stevenson (centre), Revd C. Allen (right). Churchwardens: H.C. Corke (left), J.C. Lane Andrews (behind vicar). Clerk & Sexton: S.T. Wallis (extreme right). Choirmen, left to right: W. Tyler, F. Ellis, F.W. Larcombe, W.G. Foot, H. Boorman, A. Knight, M. Watts, A. Wells. Choirboys, left to right: A. Fermor, H. Wright, A. Kealey, R. Carley, T. Dence, A. Tyler, M. Fermor, C. Bocking, G. Baker, L. Weller, B. Tompsett, E. Baker, E. Groves.

WADHURST PARISH CHURCH INTERIOR, c. 1896. The church of St Peter and St Paul celebrated its 900th anniversary in 1980, its Norman ancestry recalled in the tower masonry and other remnants behind the lectern and pulpit. There was no clear plan for subsequent enlargement, and consequently the thirteenth, fourteenth and fifteenth centuries have left the north arcade higher than the south, no column opposite its counterpart, no arches of equal span, and oddly irregular windows. But these are attractions, not detractions, for this lovely centre of worship which has survived at least six damaging lightning strikes.

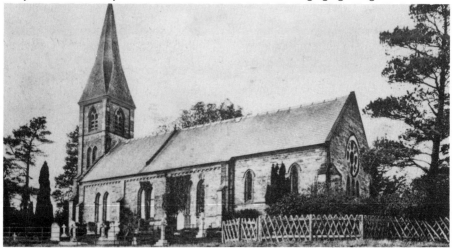

ST AUGUSTINE'S CHURCH, FLIMWELL, built by a consortium of local landowners in 1839. The architect was the renowned Decimus Burton who found fame with his distinctive terrace designs in Bloomsbury, Brighton, St Leonards and Tunbridge Wells. Flimwell was the only village church he designed. Before the spire was added in 1872 it was said the famous astronomer Sir J.F.W. Herschel used the roof of the square tower for his celestial observations; certainly it was a fact that 'Leaney's Brass Band' used to play on top of the old tower on Christmas morning and at Easter.

REVD LESLIE C. STEVENSON, chaplain to Wadhurst Hall, 1904–6, vicar of Wadhurst, 1908–20. He returned to Ireland in 1920 and in 1937 became Dean of Waterford Cathedral. He retired in 1950 and died in 1962 aged 83. His wife Lettice, although of flamboyant Irish descent, was very sympathetic to Sussex rural life and wrote a long poem about Wadhurst's tranquil lifestyle being invaded by mechanized transport.

HOSPITAL SUNDAY PARADE or, in full, 'Hospital Sunday Friendly Societies' Church Lads' and Fire Brigades' Parade', pictured in Wadhurst High Street c. 1909. It was a regular charity collection parade, often accompanied by a dog, 'Ranger', with a collection box on his back.

ORIGINALLY CALLED THE IRON CHURCH, this chapel stood in the grounds of Wick House, Woods Green, until 1898 when it was taken down and re-erected at Faircrouch Bridge and renamed the Mission Church. Charlie Bocking's grandfather used to play the harmonium there, and it had a regular congregation until the Second World War. After the war it was sold off and eventually demolished in 1956.

THE FINE OLD CHURCH AT FRANT which possibly dates back to before the twelfth century when a charter mentions 'the Chapel of Frant'. Seen to the left is the organ case which exhibits an excellent example of Frank Rosier's woodcarving skill. The organ itself is a rarity, being built in the 1870s by August Gern, once foreman to Aristide Cavaillé-Coll, greatest of French organ-builders.

THE IMMACULATELY KEPT LITTLE CHAPEL at Bells Yew Green was built in 1879 by the Countess of Huntingdon's Trust. However, chapel worship at this hamlet community is documented back to 1698 when Baptist minister Robert Norden used to come from Waldron to preach. The chapel still holds regular and well attended services.

REVD ARTHUR EDEN MA, vicar of Ticehurst for fifty-seven years from July 1851 until his death on 17 November 1908, aged 83. During his incumbency, the parish's longest, Ticehurst was virtually 'his' village, he being president or chairman of all organizations, societies and clubs, whether moral, social or athletic. Pictured with him, around 1901, is Stephen Pattenden, sexton, verger, and clerk. He died in 1918, aged 71.

ALICE JULIA EDEN, wife of the Revd Arthur Eden, in 1851. They had two sons and six daughters, one of the latter, Julia, becoming the historian of Ticehurst.

THE REVD ARTHUR EDEN pictured in 1851, shortly after his arrival in Ticehurst.

MR BONES was gardener/handyman to the Eden family.

MRS BONES (née Miss Piper from Robertsbridge) was cook to the Eden family for some thirty-five years.

A RARE RURAL TRADITION was enjoyed at Ticehurst in the 1950s and '60s when the vicar, Frank Law, conducted his Blessing of the Animals service. The vicar is depicted, in August 1962, astride Bonny, a carthorse owned by Mr C. Poland of Flimwell, and held by Kathleen Hoather. On this day some 400 people attended with 100 animals, including horses, goats, dogs, rabbits, cats, guinea pigs, mice, tortoises, and cage birds.

THE OLD VICARAGE OF TICEHURST used in Georgian and early Victorian times but clearly dating from much earlier. In fact a terrier of 21 April 1636 describes it as an 8/9 room house with barn, stall, forestall, a court, $\frac{1}{2}$ acre of garden and some 11 acres of adjoining meadowland, '... all which several parcels do abutt to the King's High Way leading from the street of Tyseherst to Wardsbrook towards the west, to a Teale and Land called Thorntons towards the North.' In 1794, about the date of this illustration, it was, according to the Revd A. Kersteman, '... delightfully situated upon a side hill, a short distance from ye church, altogether a commodious, cheerful dwelling'.

AN ENGRAVING OF TICEHURST CHURCH in 1785 from the *Gentlemen's Magazine* of 1801. The main fabric of the church is fourteenth-century, but some aisle walls are earlier indicating, perhaps, a Saxon origin. The earliest mention of a religious centre at Ticehurst occurs in a document of 1180 which speaks of 'Adam, Presbyter de Tychenherste'. It has always been well congregated and the early 1800s saw several pew rearrangements to cater for more worshippers. Substantial rebuilding took place during the Revd A. Eden's incumbency, but it had seen hard times earlier for, in 1639, the minister complained against the churchwardens for '...suffering the parrishe church to go to ruine and much decayed in lead and timber at least in a dozen places'. A rare and very early (c.1452) 'doom' window can be seen in the chancel.

THE FONT COVER AT TICEHURST CHURCH. Thought to be late fifteenth-century, only the inscription 'Elizabeth Chefe' is decipherable in the carving.

AN ANCIENT SOLID OAK DOOR in the 'Priest Chamber' over the porch of Ticehurst church. Its original key and lock are still in working order. The beams of the chamber are thought to be ship's timbers from a wreck off Rye or Hastings. The room may once have been a lock-up, hence the massive door.

THE WYBARNE BRASS IN TICEHURST CHURCH was covered up during early repairs and only rediscovered in June 1855. It commemorates John Wybarne (d. 1490), although expert opinion dates the brass a century earlier. Economy was possibly the keynote of Wybarne's internment, his surviving (second) wife Agnes arranging 'to bye a convenient stone to laye upon my husband's grave and myne'. Then what happened was that a brass now identified as no later than 1409, was 'appropriated', and fixed to the stone slab to depict the hapless Wybarne and his two consorts. Thus deduces Ticehurst historian, Julia O'Dell. Wybarne originated from a family at Hawkswell, Pembury, Kent; he owned, in his time, a large slice of Ticehurst.

REVD A. EDEN IN UNIFORM, with Long Service Medal, as chaplain to 'C' Company, 1st (Ticehurst) Cinque Ports Rifle Volunteer Corps. At his funeral a 58-strong contingent of the corps accompanied the cortège.

ZEBULON AND MRS ELLIOTT AND FAMILY, pictured around 1868. Apart from being village postman, and a cordwainer, he was thought to be the first permanent organist of Ticehurst parish church from about 1852, very likely one of the Revd Eden's appointments soon after his arrival. Zebulon Elliott died in July 1877, aged 46.

hingham, Near Church

THE VIEW OF ETCHINGHAM CHURCH from Church Lane junction, with the entrance to Mill's shop on the right. This sylvan scene is evocative of all that is valued in Wealden life, which is today precariously protected by its designation as an Area of Outstanding Natural Beauty. The date is the 1930s, and the old fellow to the extreme right is Mr Pantry, while the cricketing quartet awaiting their transport to the match are Jim Gorwyn, Chris Bull, John Morham, with umpire Joe Weston. Etchingham church was built by Sir William de Echyngham between 1360 and 1380, possibly to the design of a foreign architect, de Echyngham's tomb inscription being in Norman French. The church, once moated, has on top of its tower the original fourteenth-century weathervane in the form of the de Echyngham banner, inverted. It is accepted as the oldest such vane in the country.

TICEHURST'S FIRST WESLEYAN CHAPEL dated from 1821, being founded by James Rogers, Henry Smith, John Standen, and William Smith. It was replaced in 1840 by the bigger building depicted here, which included two schoolrooms. This too was superseded in 1897 by the building which survives today (though not as a chapel) and which cost £1,369 3s. 7d. to build.

INTERIOR OF THE WESLEYAN CHURCH which replaced the chapel in 1897. The pipe organ was added in 1902. Prior to that W.P. Dengate had been honorary organist in the old chapel for very many years. (see p. 63).

WADHURST TOWN BAND, c. 1903. Left to right: E. Tompsett, C. Piper (bandmaster), A. Manktelow, ? Cane, ? Manktelow, W. Bishop, S. Wallis, W. Piper, G. Till, W. Hubble, S. Elliott, T. Pattenden, H. Tompsett.

EDWIN MAJOR DUNGEY, a grocer by trade, came to Ticehurst by the circuitous route of the Indian Army, five years as a naval purser, Chief Clerk to the Singapore Municipality, and a business in Ilford High Street. He took over the village grocery in 1932 and only retired from it in his eighty-first year in 1951. He also founded the village fire brigade in 1933.

TICEHURST FIRE BRIGADE'S FIRST APPLIANCE, an 1880s manual pump donated by Ticehurst House, pictured in 1933.

A TWO-TON MORRIS COMMERCIAL (bought for £22 5s.) modernized the fire brigade just in time to control a potentially disastrous fire at Ticehurst Motors in 1938. The proud 'firemen' are (right) Mr Dungey and W. Picknell, pictured around 1939.

FRANK AUSTEN AND FAMILY at Marling Place, Wadhurst, in the 1880s. Left to right: Daisy, -?-, Frank, Mrs Lily Austen, Emma Skinner (nursing Harry). Miss Skinner later married and was mother of Charlie Bocking. Frank Austen was a leading figure in Wadhurst commerce being the originator of the Fat Stock Show around 1885, and its principal auctioneer until his death in 1909, at the early age of 49. He also took a prominent part in the great Trafalgar Square demonstration of 16 May 1908 when many thousands of hop traders forced a government re-think on allowing the free importation of foreign hops.

JOSEPH PANKHURST depicted in 1913, and his Flimwell Stores at the somewhat earlier date of c. 1890. Before the First World War the business also included the Welcome Stranger beerhouse.

VISIT OF THE WADHURST FARMERS' CLUB TO BRANBRIDGES MILLS (W. Arnold & Sons) at East

Peckham, Kent, on 28 June 1898. The club used to meet fortnightly at the Greyhound.

MR & MRS EVENDEN'S SADDLER'S BUSINESS at Frant, around 1904.

AN OLD TEA WRAPPING PAPER of c. 1880, used by the depicted stores. The business was started in Nelson Cottage, near the present site, by Joseph Newington in 1810. It stayed in family hands until the retirement in October 1986 of Roy Newington and his wife Pauline. Roy had joined the business in 1946, then took it over from 1962 with his wife, and sister Stella.

JABEZ SMITH'S OLD SADDLERY AND HARNESS-MAKING BUSINESS pictured probably in the 1870s. Jabez was born in 1818 at Hailsham, the eleventh of fourteen children. He moved to Wadhurst before he was thirteen and later married Elizabeth Barham, daughter of Lord and Lady Barham of Snape Wood. This building, in which he ran his saddlery business for almost fifty years (and the post office for nearly as long), remains tantalizingly undocumented. Only verbal communication, recorded by Charlie Bocking, tell us that it had once been the Old Queen's Head, of Tudor origins, but certainly it is visually identical to Smallhythe Place, near Tenterden, which dates from 1490. The Old Queen's Head was closed as an inn around 1840, at which time Jabez set up his business there and, a little later, operated the postal service from the same premises. The depicted house was demolished in 1888 and two new ones erected on the site to house the post office and the saddlers, now operated by Thomas Boyes. The latter was to marry Jabez' daughter, Polly. Jabez himself lived on to 1907, dying in his ninetieth year. (He appears on p. 128). The site of his business is today occupied by Gobles, still in the 1888 building. Would that the Victorians had chosen to preserve the Tudor one.

WILLIAM MAKEPEACE BALCOMBE became postmaster of Ticehurst in 1898 on the death of his father, G.F. Balcombe; he held the office until 1919. He was also agent for the Westminster Bank and a churchwarden from 1907 to 1916.

THE OLD POST OFFICE CUPBOARDS still *in situ* at Woodbine House, Ticehurst, in 1948, as sketched by Ruth Collingridge. They may be dated with certainty from the time when G.F. Balcombe's predecessor, William Harris, was postmaster. As the latter died in April 1878, aged 87, after running the post office for thirty years, it is quite possible that these cupboards represented the original post office for Ticehurst from the first days of nationally posted mail in c. 1840.

MARY LOUISE BALCOMBE (1860–1915), daughter of G.F. Balcombe. She helped her father in the Ticehurst post office.

MISS EMILY BALCOMBE. She helped her father, G.F. Balcombe, in the post office until she married George Newman, the postmaster at Hawkhurst. G.F. Balcombe died on 4 May 1898, aged 74. His postmastership covered the era of the mail stagecoaches which operated along the London to Hastings road and which stopped at the Hare and Hounds at Flimwell to tranship mail for these Wealden villages.

THREE WADHURST PERSONALITIES enjoying a pie and a pint at the rear of the Queen's Head around the turn of the century. They are, left to right: Mr Burke, George Tulley (licensee), Chas W. Ashby.

WILLIAM PERCY DENGATE (1879–1943). As well as founding a hairdresser's business which continues today in the same Ticehurst premises (seen below in the 1930s), Mr Dengate was also involved in many other village activities, principally clerk to the parish council, Sunday School superintendent, Day School manager, British Legion secretary, electoral roll registrar, churchwarden, and Methodist preacher.

A FINE EXAMPLE OF THE LOCAL DELIVERY TRAP that was the life blood of all village retailers as well as their outlying customers before the advent of motor vans. This smart-as-paint combination with a rare grey in harness belonged to C.W. Smith's butcher's shop that used to adjoin the Hare and Hounds inn, now the Best Beech Hotel. It is seen outside the original Cousley Wood post office, predecessor of the present one, in 1907. The deliveryman is not known.

WADHURST VOLUNTEER FIRE BRIGADE depicted around 1911 outside the fire station built by J.L. Venables. On the extreme left is Capt. C.W. Ashby, who founded the force in 1900. It was based at a site next to Sparrows Green Salvation Army hall until moving into its new one in 1911.

MR BALCOMBE'S SADDLERY SHOP in St Mary's Lane, Ticehurst. Old William Balcombe ran the business for nearly seventy years, dying on 13 July 1889 in his ninetieth year, the oldest man in the parish. His old property still stands today, though in somewhat modified form; the other houses exist virtually unchanged. The Revd A. Eden's curate, Revd G.G. Knox, lived in the house with the bay windows.

THE STAFF OF JAMES BASSETT & SONS – blacksmiths, wheelwrights, coachbuilders – pictured around 1905. Standing , left to right: E. Skinner, W. Kemp, W. Bassett, W. Watts, E. Page, W. Cork. Seated: Jack Bassett, James Bassett sen., Charles Bassett. This long-established and widely-respected business started in Sparrows Green in 1881 and then came to Durgates around 1900. The old forge was continually worked from then until 1989 when it closed to make way for modern development plans. However, in deference to the high esteem in which the business was held, the new plans for the site will leave one of the original forge buildings *in situ*, in renovated form, as part of the new complex. The founder of the business, James, died in 1940, and Will and Charles in 1936 and 1966, after which Jack continued with grandson Rodney. Jack died in 1974 aged 92 years, of which some 70 were spent in the forge.

FOLLOWING IN THE HOOFPRINTS OF OTHER SUSSEX OXEN that came to the Bassetts' forge in Durgates, the Atora grocery team is seen arriving c. 1928 for farriery attention. Oxen were shod about four or five times a year with two shoes (ox-cues) on each hoof, and the work carried out with the animal lying down with its hooves secured in a timber frame. Seen in the background is Rodney Bassett.

RODNEY BASSETT shod virtually every type of English draught animal in his Durgates forge over the years – but an elephant? In reality the photo is a clever illusion as Mr Bassett is at work on the hooves of a very small pony just visible behind him. Both animals belonged to Fossett's Circus and were inseparable friends, so when the pony needed shoeing, the elephant had to go with it. The date is about 1935, and Rodney's father looks on.

W.J. BALLARD'S COUSLEY WOOD FORGE, C. 1914. On the left is G.W. Gallup, while the boy on the right is Charles Ballard.

THE COACHBUILDING BUSINESS OF H. MORLEY pictured around 1906, with G. Gallup at left. It was located at the Old Barn, Cousley Wood.

MR G.W. GALLUP'S FORGE at Cousley Wood with George Gallup (centre) and Henry Fletcher in the doorway. The Gallup family of farriers and blacksmiths came from Waldron and first started in the Wadhurst locality at Best Beech c. 1845. George William Gallup took over the leasehold of W.J. Ballard's Cousley Wood forge in 1914, after the latter's death.

MR CORKE'S CHEMIST'S SHOP IN TICEHURST in the 1920s. In recent years it has been a hardware business, tea rooms, and is at present, a private residence.

THIS ETCHINGHAM GROCERY BUSINESS is depicted in the 1920s with George Mills (right) and his son Stan. The business continued until 1990 in the Mills family before being sold. As well as purchasing groceries there, a customer could also be measured for a suit.

THE OLD WADHURST BUTCHER'S BUSINESS depicted around 1928. It was formerly P. Smith & Co, and then H. Sayle, and E.G. Malpass, before becoming G. & J. Malpass for many years. Depicted (left) is Mr Thomas and, in the apron, H. Sayle. The delivery van is a Morris Commercial.

WADHURST CHEMIST AND VET THOMAS COUCHMAN (centre) and family outside their High Street shop decorated for the coronation of Edward VII, 1902. Also present are Thomas Boorman and family. The children are identified as Robert, Eric and Rex Boorman (the baby), with Gertie Couchman.

OSBORNE'S BAKERY, ETCHINGHAM, in the early 1900s. It was later a newsagency and post office run by Ken Smith until its later demolition and replacement by a new post office.

OSBORNE BAKERY'S (ETCHINGHAM) PRE-MOTOR VAN DELIVERY CART.

MR W. GILLHAM, fly proprietor, outside Woodbine House with his wagonette for hire, around 1892. He later had Ticehurst's first hire car, a Buick, in September 1913.

W. GILLHAM WITH MAY AND TED.

MESSRS CHEESMAN & NEWINGTON'S DELIVERY TRUCK, a solid-tyred Garner, at Wadhurst station in 1916. For new tyres the 10 m.p.h. vehicle had to go to Hastings where a firm had a special press for fitting solid tyres. Cheesman & Newington handled about 10,000 tons of coal a year through their coal wharf at the station, while through their High Street shop they were leading local traders in cereal crops, feed, and fertilizers. Depicted (right) is Charles Tompsett, with Fred King; the boy may be the young Don Griffin.

WADHURST POSTMASTER J.T. CASTERTON AND HIS STAFF, c. 1910. Back row, left to right: Bert Palmer, -?-, -?-, R.F. Wallis. Centre row: 'Shaky' Smith, G. Down, L. Humphrey, A. Cornwell, E. Hope, E. Rumens. Front row: -?-, Miss Piper, J.T. Casterton, Mrs L. Casterton, Miss Maude Casterton. Mr Casterton took over the business about this date from his father Thomas who had formerly been a navvy on the nearby railway in the 1850s.

W. BALDWIN'S GARAGE AT DURGATES around 1905. The business was taken over by G.W. Pritchard in 1933 and traded as Pritchards until 1989, when the site was sold for redevelopment. Seated in some of the modern cars of the day are, left to right: William Baldwin, Frank Newington, Walter Baldwin, John Gibbons, Miss Verona and Miss Ann Baldwin. In the expert opinion of motoring historian Michael Worthington-Williams of Dyfed, some of the car makes are: Darracqs at extreme left and centre: a Swift second from right, with possibly a De Dion far right.

COOPER'S STORES, TICEHURST, around 1888, with the pentice roof outside supported by cast-iron columns — almost identical to the frontage today, a century on.

THE COOPER'S STORES DELIVERY CART, depicted around 1914.

THE STAFF OF FRANT POST OFFICE depicted in the early 1900s. The original site was adjacent to that pictured and comprised a modest wooden structure which, in time, expanded to two (unsafe) storeys. The building depicted then took over the role. A notable postmaster between the First and Second World War was Frank Rosier, although the primary claim to fame of this 'Sussex Grinling Gibbons' was his ecclesiastical wood carvings, mostly in Frant, but also ornamenting several other Sussex churches.

THE BUSINESS PREMISES OF W.A. SKINNER were formerly at the Marlpit area of Durgates, Wadhurst. This photograph was found deliberately laid under the floor timbers of the new building (today Gobles) that replaced the old post office and saddlers business in 1888. With the photo was a piece of wood inscribed 'This house build for Jabesh Smith by W.A. Skinner in the year (1888) Agust the 1st, floor layed August 1st A. Skinner'. The spelling is original. Those depicted are not known but the man on the upper floor could be Walter Atkins Skinner himself. The beautifully square-cut joinery of their workshop pays its own tribute to their woodworking skill.

TOM JARRETT AT DOWNASH GARAGE, FLIMWELL, with, on his right, a Renault limousine, and, on his left, a Mercedes. The date is about 1907.

MARTIN'S FARM MILK ROUND DELIVERY, pictured near Frant around 1912, with Percy Motherwick driving.

THIS LONG-ESTABLISHED TICEHURST BUSINESS is represented by (left to right) Norman Field, Reg Field and Alec Pilbeam. The date is about 1926, and the group is completed by 'Gin' the dog.

THE FIELDS AND FRIENDS, in 1926. Standing, left to right: J. Maynard, W.J. Field. In front row: R. Field, Mrs Bullock, Mrs R. Field (son Harold on her knee), Mrs W.J. Field, and A.E. Maynard.

MEMBERS OF THE MARYAN FAMILY collecting linen from the old White Hart at Wadhurst for their 'Spion Kop' laundry at Jonas Lane. The man holding the horse is Mr Page, son of George Page, licensee of the White Hart, who died in 1893. The driver is possibly Frank Maryan, with James in the centre. This White Hart was next to Newington's newsagent until 1921 when it crossed the road to rename the Spotted Cow as the White Hart, still there today.

WADHURST VOLUNTEER FIRE BRIGADE on their Dennis appliance celebrating the Peace Declaration of 19 July 1919. The driver is A. Everest with, alongside, W.H. Newington.

THE FRANT XI, pictured on their Green in 1869. A rare, very early village cricket photograph; the earliest known at Lords is 1857. Like the majority of High Weald wickets, Frant Green has a pronounced slope, though here somewhat disguised by the camera angle. The Green still continues as Frant CC ground, being only a short stroll from the comfortable George inn (the home of this photograph) where many a close match is replayed at the bar. Recorded cricket on Frant Green goes back to 1825.

ETCHINGHAM AND FONTRIDGE CRICKET CLUB in the 1930s. Surnames only known. Standing, left to right: Santer, Wells, Hayward, Catt, Harris, Roff, Catt, Hallett, Baker. Seated: Funnell, Mewett, Bolton, Mewett sen., Tester. An early mention of Etchingham cricketers occurs in July 1813 when, with Robertsbridge, they took on Brede, Westfield, and 'Seddlescomb'.

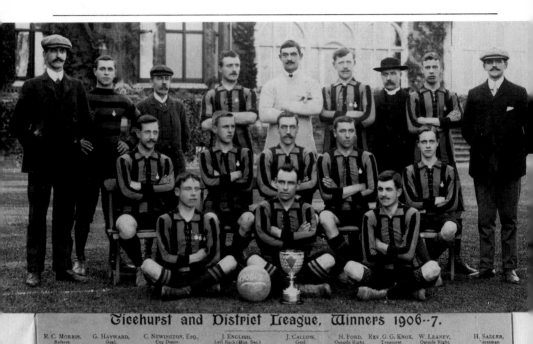

Ticehurst and District League, Winners 1906-7.

| R. C. MORRIS, Referee. | G. HAYWARD, Goal. | C. NEWINGTON, ESQ., Cup Donor. | J. ENGLISH, Left Back (Hon. Sec.) | J. CALLOW, Goal. | H. FORD, Outside Right. | REV. G. G. KNOX, Treasurer. | W. LEANEY, Outside Right. | H. SADLER, Linesman. |

| H. W. CORNWELL, Inside Right. | E. ROBERTS, Centre Forward. | F. MILES, Centre Half. | A. JUDGE, Inside Left. | A. AYLARD, Outside Left. |

| A. AYLARD, Right Half. | A. P. ACOTT, Right Back (Captain). | E. CHEESMER, Left Half. |

ORGANIZED FOOTBALL IN TICEHURST appears to have been started around 1890 by R.C. Morris and the curate, Revd G.G. Knox. The first match in Ticehurst seems to have been against Burwash on 21 February 1891 when Ticehurst lost 3–1. The team formed itself into a club in 1895 and then went from strength to strength. As well as winning the depicted trophy, they were winners of the Tunbridge Wells League in 1899/1900, its first year, and again ten years later. Since these beginnings the Ticehurst footballers have acquitted themselves honourably and successfully in many competitions. Before the First World War Dr Newington used to fly the club colours from his carriage when on his rounds, but possibly the club's most famous tradition was its uniquely rigorous practice programme, as recorded in an 1891 parish magazine: 'Wednesdays, at 5.30; Saturdays, at 5 o'clock; all moonlight nights; and twice a week, just before sunrise till 7.'

THE WADHURST WEDNESDAY FOOTBALL TEAM, around 1910. Standing, left to right: A. Gadd, C. Baldwin, F. Watts, -?-, -?-, A. Hunnisett, Mr Meredith(?), T. Griffin. Seated: Mr Bateman(?), W.G. Anderson, W. Lofts, Will Newington, C. Pomfret. Seen at extreme top left is the old Spotted Cow pub which preceded the White Hart on the site. The name change took place in 1921. The long low roof extending back from the pub may be the indoor rifle range which was adjacent to it.

JOE DAVIS giving an exhibition of billiards and snooker at the Wadhurst Social Club on 21 September 1949. Some of the onlookers are, left to right: F. Piper, J. Burgess, G. Meech, F. Keel, J. Bishop, C. Bloomfield, E. Gill, A.W.G. McQueen and, with the cue, Harold Terry, a noted Tonbridge amateur.

THE TICEHURST CROQUET CLUB around the time of its foundation in 1919. Standing, left to right: Mrs Bullock, Mrs Maynard, Miss V. Woodroffe, Mrs Pilbeam, Revd Martin, Mrs Cooper, Mrs W. Woodroffe. Seated: Mrs W.J. Field, Mr F. Field. The lawn used was the old Bowling Green originally laid out in 1906 to the east of the Institute. At a later date the sole croquet venue was the Vicarage lawn.

WADHURST V JARVIS BROOK 3.3.06

THIS MATCH is taking place at Wadhurst on the old football field known as 'Carpenter's Field'. The football club appears to have joined the cricket club on the other side of Washwell Lane around 1922, when the Hall & Field Trust took over the field behind the Institute. (The cricket club had used the latter field since the 1870s.)

WADHURST TENNIS CLUB MEMBERS in 1934. Left to right: Gertie Couchman, Mrs Vidler, Miss Casterton, Mrs K. Newington, Dr E.A.C. Fazan, Revd Causton, Mrs Davis, Minnie Wallis, Mr Davis, Mr Foot, Mr Orpin, Mr Wright, Betty Ratcliff, Mr Turley, Mr Howell, H.C. Bocking, Mr & Mrs Meech. At rear: Miss D. Cutbush, Gladys Watts, Miss B. Bocking, Doris Baldwin, George Mitchell, E. Bidlake, Jack Casterton, Mrs Howell, Winnie Larcombe, Gladys Larcombe.

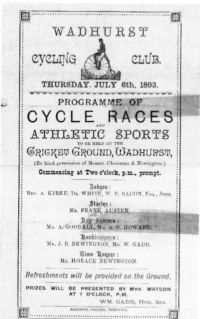

TWENTY-ONE DIFFERENT COMPETITIVE EVENTS took place at this meeting, with musical intervals provided by the Wadhurst Brass Band and the Wadhurst Drum and Fife Band.

THE WADHURST CYCLING CLUB aboard a variety of machines, pictured around 1887, perhaps not long after its foundation. The club was based at the Queen's Head, and seems to have been started largely through the efforts of J.B. Newington. An early chairman was Frank Austen.

HENRY BOORMAN, Wadhurst cricketer for over forty years, captain from 1896 to 1924. His son Cecil continued the tradition by serving the club as player and official from 1920 to 1965. Given his chance, Cecil Boorman might well have been a county player, such was the standard of his game.

W.G. GRACE'S YOUNGEST SON, CHARLES, also played for Wadhurst for some ten seasons. He headed the batting averages in 1925 and later, in 1932, topped the bowling with his tricky underarm lobs.

A. CARPENTER,		S. SMITH,		H. T. S. CHANNING,		W. B. BACON, Esq.,		W. MANWARING,		J. VINCENT,	
Referee.		Hon. Sec.		Right Half.		V. President.		Left Back.		Lineman.	
VIDLER,		H. BOORMAN,		W. ROSS-BROWN,		H. BACON,		F. SKERRETT,		F. MORRIS,		J. HIDE,
de R. Fd.		Outside R. Fd.		Right Back.		(Capt.) Centre Half.		Outside L. Fd.		Centre Fd.		Left Half.
			C. NOAKES,				FRED. SKERRETT,					
			Inside L. Fd.				Goal.					

FEW FOOTBALLING FRATERNITIES can claim as early a mention as Wadhurst. Thirteen persons were fined for playing the game there in 1548. The descendants of these troublesome Tudors formed themselves into a club in 1884 and, as pictured in 1895, were not long in starting a useful silver collection, namely the Tunbridge Wells Charity Cup. Later years saw them win the depicted trophy again (in 1976), and in the same year the Sussex Intermediate Cup, then in 1980 they became Southern Counties League Champions. In 1971 the players achieved additional fame by playing non-stop for 18 hours, so setting a new record in the Guinness Book of Records, and benefiting a charity at the same time.

Bottom, left:
WADHURST CRICKETERS c. 1907. Standing, left to right: J. Hubble, S.T. Wallis, -?-, G. Tulley, J. Selby. Seated: Owen Newington, H.E. Boorman. Front: H.C. Bocking, E. Wickenden. Umpire: G. Down. The telegraph probably indicates a record team score, maybe the reason for the photograph. Interestingly, the club record at the time of writing stands only a little higher at 274 for 3. Wadhurst can claim, probably, the oldest cricketing associations in the locality, their documentary archives going back to 1758. Naturally, in this long course of time many matches and players of distinction hold a permanent place in the club records. Not least the village tailor, Silas Cooper, who in 1805 at Thomas Lord's original ground as a member of a national invitation team, took the wickets of eight of the best English batsmen in one innings.

INAUGURATION OF THE WADHURST BOWLS CLUB on 2 June 1934. The club was created by C.B. Mould, F. Ratcliff and W. Grinham in October 1933, the pavilion being supplied by Mr A.E. Parke. Sir George Courthope presided at the official opening and the first match was against Frant. Clifford Mould won the singles championship and, with H. Kemp, the pairs cup in the opening season and continued winning trophies up to 1974, his eightieth year. At least half a dozen club players have represented the county. Seated, left to right: -?-, F. Bond, H.C. Corke, F. Ratcliff, Lord Courthope, Mr Luck, C.B. Mould, C.W. Grinham, M. Watts. Second row: Mr Clements, -?-, Mr Everest, Mr Ballard, Mr Stemp (behind). At the back: A. Parks (in cloth cap), Mr Piper (centre), Revd Causton, S. Wallis, G. Meech.

A HAPPY TIDEBROOK & BEST BEECH FC celebrating the winning of the Tunbridge Wells League Div. 3 championship of 1932/3. Standing, left to right: W. Palmer, J. Potter, E. Farmer, F. Hemsley, P. Heasman, C. Palmer, F. Palmer, Mr Griffin. Front row: B. Athey, B. Reeves, R. Hayward, L. Gamlin, P. Ross.

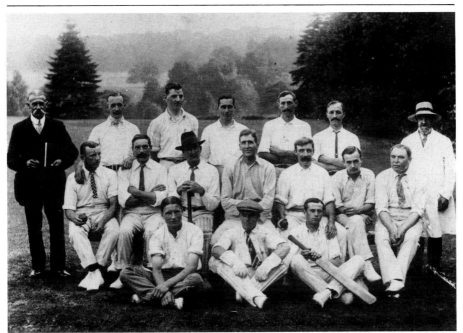

BAYHAM CRICKET CLUB, 1914. Back row, left to right: -?-, -?-, G. Spackman, A. Sands, ? Sands. Middle row: Mr Haken (scorer), J. Kennard, Mr Barham, W. Crump, Revd Jose, J. Waters, O. Haken, J. Stockley, D. Lambert (umpire). Front row: -?-, T. Herring, A. Crump.

A SPORTING AFTERNOON at Wadhurst around 1910, possibly the annual Amateur Athletic Sports held in 'Mr Leney's Field, Stone Cross'. Left to right: E.D. May, Mr Maryan, A. Crust, -?-, P. Lavender, -?-, E. Hope, P. Manktelow, C.W. Ashby.

STEP STILE, the path taken by hundreds of Wadhurst children as they made their way past Wadhurst church to Pell Hill School. Of those depicted, the known identities are: Violet Wallis (girl at top), Charity Farebrother (girl with hat), Bob Keeley (boy between the girls).

DALE HILL HOUSE, HOLLYBANK, TICEHURST, around 1893. The group are thought to be, back row, left to right: Fred Baldwin, Lizzie Rootes, Mrs Baldwin (with Kate), Mrs Vidler. Front row: Francis, Florrie, Annie, John, and Edith Baldwin.

SEACOX HEATH, FLIMWELL, around 1870. The house originally occupying the site was built in 1745 by Arthur Grey, one-time leader of the infamous Hawkhurst Gang of smugglers, known locally as the Sea Cocks. The law eventually caught up with Arthur Grey and he was transported to Australia. The depicted mansion, designed by William Slater, was built for Lord Goschen, Governor of Madras, and perhaps more famous for his role as the British Ambassador in Germany in 1914 when the 'scrap of paper' diplomatic incident occurred. Seacox Heath was sold to the Soviet Trade Delegation in 1946.

WILLIAM THE CONQUEROR is said to have re-shod his horses after the Battle of Hastings by this well at Shoyswell, depicted c. 1908. To commemorate this tradition, the arms of the Shoyswell family are three silver horseshoes.

SHOYSWELL MANOR, between Ticehurst and Etchingham, dates mostly from the seventeenth century. The lands can, however, be dated back to before the Conquest when 'Bishop Alric held it in fee of King Edward. There were $4\frac{1}{2}$ hides ... land for 9 ploughs, a church and woodland ... it was worth 114 shillings. It was laid waste.' The latter comment was applied by the contemporary chroniclers to many Wealden settlements as the 1066 invasion swept across the county.

THE TICEHURST WEDDING of Dr Taylor's daughter, Marion, to Mr B. Bennett, a schoolmaster from Paignton. The date is 24 August, 1892. Ruth Collingridge gives the identities as follows: Seated, left to right: Mrs Eden, -?-, Miss Swan, Mr Swan, Mrs Bennett, Dr Taylor, the bride, the groom, Mrs Taylor, -?-, Mrs Swan. Standing: -?-, Miss Hopkins, Alice Clark, Revd G.G. Knox, Carrie Clark, -?-, Miss Swan, Mr Swan, Miss L. Taylor, Revd A. Eden, L. Taylor, Revd Eagleton (Flimwell), -?-, Miss Julia Eden, Mrs Holdsworth, Mr Aitkens, Dr Digby, Miss Eagleton, Miss Barton, Miss Barton.

THE LATEST MODEL, A PANHARD, at Sparrows Green Corner, Wadhurst, around 1904. The driver is not identified unfortunately. The car was a four-cylinder, 12 hp machine, with water-cooled hydraulic brake system.

FRANCIS McCLEAN, the pilot of this plane, was a pioneering aviator of the early 1900s who founded, in 1911, the first naval flying school in Britain. This aircraft, forced down at Earls Farm near Wadhurst by bad weather in 1912, is a Short Tractor Biplane S.36, one of McClean's private fleet of sixteen aircraft. He had a series of gold tie-pins, each fashioned after the aircraft and balloons he had flown. Mr McClean was knighted in 1926 for services to aviation.

PARTICIPANTS IN A GRAND FÊTE at Wadhurst on 16 July 1930. The theme was 'Young Farmers'. The only known identities are Miss C. Tompsett (Mrs Lee) at right, and Bob Watts, front centre in white shirt, holding a corn sheaf. The fine old Sussex wagon of Cheesman & Newington was almost certainly constructed at Bassett's coach-building business at Durgates.

Wadhurst Hall.

A SALE PROSPECTUS of 1944 described Wadhurst Hall as comprising 'Hall and Grand Staircase, Ballroom, Winter Garden, nine reception and living rooms, twenty-four bed and dressing rooms, with nursery suite and staff rooms, Private Chapel, Riding School, Clubhouse, Laundry, and one room fitted specially for King Edward VII (when Prince of Wales).' Long before this time a house, then called Hightown, on the same site, had belonged to one of the wealthiest local families, the Maunser ironmasters. The depicted house was built in 1797 by John Baker. Later occupants included the de Murrietas, close friends of the royal family; they ensured the royal suite mentioned above also catered for the occasional presence of Lily Langtry. The owner from 1899 to 1927 was Julius Drewe, joint founder of the Home & Colonial Stores. After changing hands in 1928 the house was renamed Wadhurst Park, and twenty years later it was demolished.

HAREMERE HALL, 'Time rich house, half hidden, lovingly lived in'. The mellow façade and secluded setting of the hall outside Etchingham belie a past of some incident. Its occupancy can be dated back to Miles de Haremere (or Heremere) at the end of the twelfth century when he was lord of the manor. By the time of the Stuarts it had become a comfortable country house and, at the outbreak of the Civil War, was lived in by the Busbridge family. During the disturbances a roving patrol of Cromwell's soldiers arrived at the house one night and when Colonel Busbridge answered their knock on the door he was shot dead on his own doorstep. The consequence of this event upon the house is recounted some two centuries later by another visitor, the artist Henry Corbould: 'I would tell how that I have seen his bedroom which he left that morning and saw things as he left them, except for the dilapidations by the Owls, etc. The domestics had strict orders never to touch the room. The effect upon me was something strange, I admit, to see the result of a couple of centuries of dust, all that remained on the floor beneath the oak pegs on which the Colonel had left his hat and clothes, after the moths had done their worst upon them. The Sneppe family seem to have had a species of respect and certainly avoided molesting things there. I suppose I must have been wanting in proper respect for I constantly rummaged up there and found all sorts of curious things some of which must have rested there for fully four centuries, such as boar spears, hunting spears, fire dogs time of Henry V (1413–1422), oak chairs with stamped leather seats of Cromwell's date, a beautifully printed in arabesque-work bedstead which had been used by the maidservants, time of Henry VIII, and other quaint bedsteads such as are seen at Hampton Palace and Knole. A large chest used to stand at the top of the grand staircase with lots of papers and parchments.' (Corbould MSS.) All this was before the MacLean family moved in during the 1840s. After their restorations, Corbould enquired of the architect about the preserved Cromwellian room and associated Tudor furniture and fittings; the reply said '. . . they had been burnt as useless lumber'. So much for the nineteenth-century zeal for the restoration of things artistic and archaic! How unique would that room have been today! (Henry Corbould went on to his own niche in history – he designed the Penny Black stamp; his grave and memorial are in Etchingham church.) The current occupant of Haremere, Lady Killearn, widow of the former British Ambassador in Cairo, has cared for the house over the last four decades.

"Pashley", Ticehurst.

PASHLEY AT TICEHURST goes back to the de Passele family of c. 1206, the earliest surviving deed being of 1317 when Sir Edmund de Passele had Charter of Free Warren over lands in Ticehurst. The present building dates from Tudor times, being owned by Sir James Boleyn (uncle of Ann), but was much rebuilt in 1612 by Anthony May, Sheriff of Sussex and Ironmaster. May's family and descendants owned Pashley from 1540 to 1922.

THE WETHERALL FAMILY were principal occupants of Pashley in the Victorian years, Nathan Wetherall, 1808–87, (pictured) coming there in 1863. His father, Richard, an army man, successfully defended Pashley with pistol and drawn sword against the agricultural rioters who, in 1830, tried to wreck the estate's new threshing machine.

WADHURST CASTLE, after being destroyed by fire in October 1933. This largely Victorian mansion stood on the site of the ancient property of Maplehurst which dated from the fourteenth century. It assumed its castellated form in 1818, being then progressively enlarged until reaching its depicted proportions in the 1870s. Before its demise and the consequent break-up of the estate, Wadhurst Castle encompassed some 465 acres, including Foxe's Farm, Snape Wood, Birchett's Wood, Hope Cottage, Stone Cross Farm and Durgates Lodge.

MISS JULIA A. EDEN, daughter of the Revd Arthur Eden, and joint author with Leonard J. Hodson LLB of *Ticehurst; the story of a Sussex Village*, 1925. She married H.F.C. O'Dell on 19 September 1911, and died in 1955 aged 90.

THE PRINCE OF WALES (later Edward VII), standing fourth from right, with friends at Wadhurst Hall in the 1890s. The cost of upgrading their house to a standard suitable for frequent royal house parties led to the bankruptcy of the de Murietta family and their eventual sale of Wadhurst Hall in 1899.

MERRIAMS, THE GRAVEL PIT, TICEHURST. A fine example of a Sussex farmhouse that has been continually added to over the centuries. The old gentleman at the door may be John Noakes who died in November 1881, aged 60. Prior to the Noakes family, the house was for many years occupied by the Eagles (or Egles) family.

GEORGE SMITH, roadman, a grand old man of Wadhurst.

GEORGE ROGERS at the local Hospital Sunday collection stall on Etchingham station, June 1920. The identity of the railwayman was not known to the donor of the photograph.

A GROUP OF ETCHINGHAM WORTHIES, pictured around 1920, and probably wearing the Order of Buffaloes regalia. Most identities are known. Standing, left to right: Ernie Weston, Jack Cady, Tom Croft, Frank Ballard, -?-, Mr Catt, George Rogers, Jim Bolton, Ted Turner, Charlie Relf, Jack Jones, Ernie Foster, Fred Kemp. Seated: Tom Guest, Herbert Eastwood, George Watkins, -?-.

FRED TURNER, sisters Eva and Mary, and brothers Harry and Ted, at Manor Farm hop gardens near Frant, c. 1902.

OLD BAYHAM (ONCE BEGHAM) ABBEY between Wadhurst and Lamberhurst, established c. 1200 by the Premonstratensian Order. Though ostensibly an order devoted to silence and solitude, the Bayham fraternity attracted so much attention by riotous behaviour, both within and without its gates, over the centuries that its dissolution in the 1530s was only remarkable in having been so long delayed.

BOARZELL, TICEHURST, from a watercolour by S.H. Grimm of 1783. The house depicted, once moated, was demolished in 1859, having been the home of the Roberts family for some three centuries. The manor of 'Baresselle' is traceable to the twelfth century and earlier owners included the lords of Etchingham, and the de Haremere family. (Courtesy British Museum)

A CHRISTMAS FAMILY GATHERING at Gibbs Reed Farm, Ticehurst, in 1895. Back row, left to right: Archie Butler, Fred Fox, Charlie Morris, Elsie Pont, Harold Butler, Eva Butler, Denis Snatt, Walter Butler. Middle row: Marie Field, Gertie Fox (with Winnie), Alice Morris (with Gertie), George Pont, Mary Pont, Lilian Snatt (with Madge), Topsie Butler. Front row: Alice Butler, Violet Butler, Muriel Pont, Sidney Snatt, Cecil Snatt, Bessie Pont.

A BOXING DAY SHOOT for the men at Gibbs Reed Farm, Ticehurst, in 1895. Left to right: Charlie Morris, Harold Butler, George Pont, Walter Butler, Archie Butler, Denis Snatt, Fred Fox.

WHILIGH, between Wadhurst and Ticehurst, around 1952. The estate belonged to the de Curtehopes from about 1255, and then to the Courthopes from 1513 until the death of the last Baron Courthope in 1955. Oak from Whiligh was expressly requested by King Richard II in 1394 for building the roof of his Westminster Hall, the largest of its kind in the world.

RT. HON. SIR GEORGE LOYD COURTHOPE, Baron Courthope of Whiligh Bt, PC, MC, TD, DL, JP. A leading national authority on forestry management, he served in the Forestry Commission for 21 years and was joint founder of the English Forestry Commission in 1911. He was MP for Rye from 1906 to 1945, and elevated to the peerage in 1948. His Military Cross was won in the fateful Aubers Ridge action of 9 May 1915, when so many villagers serving in the Royal Sussex Regiment lost their lives. Lord Courthope, last holder of the title, died in 1955, aged 78.

A TYPICALLY MASSIVE WHILIGH OAK TRUNK, probably destined for the repairs to Westminster Hall in 1924. On the left Walter Baldwin, with Fred Sweatman.

TREE FELLING ON WHILIGH. The family of Frank Kemp, the foreman (extreme right), worked on the Whiligh estate for over 150 years. He himself lived at Moseham for 40 years.

THOMAS HOLFORD AND HIS SON BENJAMIN, with 'Boxer', at their woodyard near Frant, in the early 1920s. Thousands of such woodyard businesses have thrived over the centuries on the timber of the High Weald.

Oxen at Work in Sussex.

A TYPICAL WEALDEN FOUR-OXEN TEAM for road haulage, around 1906. For heavy field ploughing, five or six animals would be hitched together. The reason oxen were more suited for draught work on the Weald was that in the viscous clay of the area their hooves expanded under weight, and then contracted for easy withdrawal. The team and wagon depicted here is virtually identical to those that were working the land when King William's Domesday revenue men were visiting and valuing Wealden farms.

THE EASTWOOD BROTHERS collecting in the hops at Burgham Farm, Etchingham. The farm was owned by the Newington family; the latter are able to document their local descendancy back to Sir Adam de Newington in 1481.

A VIEW OF BARTLEY MILL, Bells Yew Green, before 1886 when the road seen was re-routed a short distance away to cross the then new bridge.

HOP PICKERS passing through Bells Yew Green *en route* to the hop gardens that lay around Bartley Mill. Albert Ingerfield is leading the team which is pulling a fine example of the Sussex wagon.

HOP PICKING at John Luxford's Foxhole Farm, Wadhurst. Left to right: Mr Fuller, Gwen Luxford, Alice Newington, Mrs Greagsby, Lily Luxford, John Luxford, Alice Skinner, -?-, -?-. At this date, around the 1880s, the pickers earned about 1s. for 8 bushels.

ANIMATED ACTIVITY IN FRANT HIGH STREET, around June 1913.

THE OLD WADHURST BREWERY PREMISES of Wright & Sons at Durgates at the turn of the century. Originally, in mid-Victorian times, called the Holmesdale Brewery, it became 'Gregory Wright, Brewer & Aerated Water Manufacturer'. Sited near Bassett's forge, old Jack Bassett recalled it selling beer at 1s. a gallon to carters waiting while their horses were shod. It closed in October 1913 when O.T. Corke bought it to use as a War Work Depot. Pictured is Dick Rabson (left) with the Wright brothers.

WADHURST FAT STOCK SHOW OFFICIALS, 1928. On rear rostrum, left to right: G.G. Gallup, R. Vidler, T.R. Boorman, R.A. Boorman, B. Ferguson. In front: R. Manby, H.P. Lee (& friend), L. Sewell, T. Boorman, R. Brissenden, C. Morris, J. Sands, C. Golding, W. Gadd, A. Gibb, L. Gibb, W. Anderson, W. Sands, F. Harris, C.H. Bocking, C. Ensoll, -?-, D. Griffin, J. Dowden, O. Lemmon, C. Burnell, A. Gutsell, W. Bassett. No clear starting date for this show is at present known. The most certain references to 'a Market' exist as far back as 1852, but perhaps refer to the fortnightly corn sales held on Tuesdays at the Greyhound. The first definite dating of a 'stock' show occurs in 1888. It may have been originated by a Mr Durrant of Welshes Farm, Ticehurst, but soon after was run by Frank Austen of Marling Place. The highly popular show became known as the Wadhurst Christmas Fat Stock Show and continued for every year (except during the wars) from 1888 to 1982. It was then moved to Heathfield due to problems of vehicle access to the old market premises. This removal ended a continuous market tradition in Wadhurst of 729 years. It had started with the grant by Henry III in 1253 of a charter (the original still survives) to hold a market each Saturday together with a fair on 29 June each year. Thus Wadhurst was technically a market town rather than a village. The fair was still a popular attraction in Georgian times and clearly had memories for Walter Gale, inebriate diarist and sometime Mayfield schoolmaster who, in 1750, '... took a turn in the fair where on sweethearts and maidenheads I laid out 2d.' The Show was still going a century later but '... the Market House, a small quadrangular building, which for the honour of the Town is kept in good repair, altho' never used', was noted by William Courthope. This structure stood just outside the present surgery and had a tiled roof supported by iron rods on a 4 ft wall. The market building used until 1982 was an old corrugated iron Tunbridge Wells church re-erected at Wadhurst in 1900. Standing just south of the High Street, it doubled as a function hall until the Commemoration Hall assumed the later role from 1922. Until recently an extremely old cruck-roofed barn which was last used as a slaughterhouse existed behind the butchers just along from the market site. Its antiquity was never proven before its 1980s demolition but, just maybe, it was a last structural link with the medieval market?

LOADING HOP POCKETS at Overy's Farm, Ticehurst, around 1913. Note the orchard ladder to the left of the picture.

SAMUEL BALDWIN, brother of George Baldwin who farmed Norwoods Farm. Samuel was landlord of the Railway Tavern at Wadhurst station from 1878 and also ran a horse-bus service between Ticehurst and Wadhurst. The late Charlie Bocking thought that Samuel Baldwin formerly ran the Greyhound until Jacob Pitt took it over in 1856, and then moved to the Tunnel Hotel, Durgates, before acquiring the Railway Hotel.

A PARTY OF BEATERS at a Bayham Abbey shoot, probably around 1860. The dark colour of some of the smock collars is red; the children were also wearing red jackets.

AN EXAMPLE OF A TRADITIONAL SUSSEX SMOCK from the pattern book of the Ticehurst Women's Institute. Since its foundation under the presidency of Lady Julian Parr in 1918, the Ticehurst WI, has included instruction in basket making, skin curing, folk dancing, needlework and knitting as well as smock making. Ticehurst smocks were famous and exported to many countries, especially following their display at the London WI Exhibition between the wars. There were strict rules for smock wearing, with specific types for weekdays and weekends. Today 'smock lore' is best studied at Warnham Cottage, East Hoathly, where the traditional craft is kept alive and well. A typical Ticehurst smock of c. 1938 is displayed in the church.

JACK SMITH, seated, at New Houses, Frant, around 1902, with Fred and Eva Turner.

DANIEL LEANEY, foreman at Walters Farm, Ticehurst, with his family depicted around 1893. The children are, left to right, Sophy, Ruth, Eliza, Frederick, and Harry.

MR & MRS GEORGE BALWIN of Norwoods Farm, Ticehurst. He died in 1894.

ALBERT BALDWIN carrying hopsacks through the hop gardens of Norwoods Farm which he ran after the death of his father, George.

A PRIME SUSSEX HEIFER on Frank Austen's estate at Marling Place, in the care of stockman Charles Dunmall. The latter was the caretaker of the old Market Hall from 1900 where the stock auctions took place. The photograph probably dates from 1905.

THRESHING BY STEAM in the 1890s at New House Farm, Sheepstreet Lane, Etchingham. The identities were not known to the donor of the photograph, unfortunately.

MRS LUCY INGERFIELD (left) fetching water from a well near Bartley Mill. In 1935 there were nearly 100 parishes, from a total of about 600 in Sussex, Kent and Surrey, without a piped water supply, and of these, two-thirds were in Sussex. Professor S.W. Wooldridge, writing about the local geology in 1953, said, 'The Weald has long been a land of wells and, in controlling the sites of these, geology made its greatest contribution to determining the settlement pattern of the area.'

THE OLD LEAFWOOD BREWERY when it was sited on the outskirts of Bells Yew Green; today the premises are occupied by Ward's Mobility Services Ltd. The brewery continued under the care of the Ware family until 1954 when it was taken over by Flowers of Stratford-upon-Avon, later being sold to Ward's who perpetuated the tradition by retaining the name Ware Works.

PASTORAL SERENITY at Bartley Mill, Bells Yew Green, in the 1920s. This corn mill, dating from at least the thirteenth century, has rarely been idle, being worked over the centuries by some of the most notable local Sussex families. The family living there today, Piers and Amanda Garnham, have restored the mill to full working order and produce bread, specialist flours, and a variety of other home-grown products. It had lain idle since 1904 before being re-opened on 4 April 1987, and now the results of their considerable joint labours, aided by millwright Peter Stenning, are open to public display all the year round.

DRAWING HOP SAMPLES AT LITTLE PELL FARM, Wadhurst, in 1905. Left to right: G. Mitten jun., G. Mitten sen., Jabez Smith, Rowland Smith (the tenant farmer), Nicholas Barham, Frederick Griffiths.

HOP PICKING AT LITTLE PELL FARM at the turn of the century. Seated centre is Jabez Smith, longtime postmaster and saddler to Wadhurst, on the left is Mrs Ansell and, on the right, Mrs Newman.

GEORGE MITTEN feeding and pressing hops at Little Pell.

MEASURING THE HOPS AT LITTLE PELL, with W. Pierson holding the measure.

THE OLD CREAMERY that stood adjacent to Etchingham station, where the milk collected from local farms was cooled prior to sending it by rail to London. At about this date, the 1920s, the creamery was run by the ubiquitous George Rogers.

RISEDEN WINDMILL, TIDEBROOK, went out of use before 1910, the last miller being Mr G. White. Newton Tompsett of Wenbans recalled using the mill when he was fifteen in around 1898.

FLIMWELL WINDMILL around 1865. Mr Weston, the miller, is carrying his hopper.

THE OLD FLIMWELL WINDMILL being pulled down in 1902 by Mr Barfoot and Will Colvin, with the assistance of some thirty-three horses.

MARK CROSS WINDMILL before and after the fire of 1911. Originally built in 1760, it was rebuilt again after the fire but was converted to a house in 1960.

BAKERS FARM, THREE LEGGED CROSS, TICEHURST, around 1868. Outside are, left to right: Edward Field sen., Edward Field jun., William Field, Frederick Field. The farmhouse, festooned with white grapevine, is a rural rarity, its continuous-jetty construction more usually found in urban environments. Documents describing the property go back to 1467.

HOP WASHING AT OVERY'S FARM, TICEHURST, in 1902. The merry band of workers are, left to right: Will Brown jun., Sam Clarke, Joseph Piper, Albert Warham, William Brown (foreman) and John Adams.

DUNSTERS MILL, TICEHURST, c. 1910. It had been worked as a water cornmill since the late fourteenth century. During the Napoleonic invasion scare of 1801–3 the mill was listed in the militia returns as of strategic importance as a corn supply source. A later long-term family of millers were the Huntleys, followed by the Orpins, of whom William built a steam engine to work the machinery. In the mid-1970s, when the new reservoir of Bewl Water was being planned, the mill was in danger of inundation. The owner, Hubert Beale, petitioned Parliament to save the building and was successful in winning an order to have the mill dismantled, brick by brick, and re-erected some half a mile away, above the high water mark.

A DRAWING OF A TYPICAL WEALDEN GUN FORGE. Processes shown are: charcoal loading at top, chipping clean a complete casting, and lowering a mould into a gun-pit. The water wheel powering the forge machinery can be seen below the stylized oak forest. (Courtesy WIRG)

PART OF THE OLD SNAPE IRON MINE WORKINGS near Wadhurst. Wealden iron-ore had been worked into implements for centuries before Julius Ceasar attempted to penetrate the great southern forests in 55 BC. This photograph depicts the last resting place of that same industry, some 2,000 years later. During the Hastings railway construction of the 1850s ore beds were located 'just west of the 53rd milestone'. A mine was opened in August 1857 and operated for a year sending ore to Staffordshire by rail, before closing as uneconomic. It was the last resurgence of the ancient industry that had made the Weald the 'Black Country' of the eighteenth century. The depicted gallery is some 150 yd long and leads on to several others. The photograph dates from 1936 when the workings were last surveyed before final sealing off.

THE MOST ENDURING MONUMENT to the old ironmasters of the High Weald 'Black Country' exists in Wadhurst parish church in the form of some thirty iron memorial slabs set in the floor. Pictured left, in the foreground is one for William Barham of 'Scrage Oake', died 6 November 1701; and, below, the one for John Barham of 'Shoosmithes', who died 5 December 1648. Other Sussex churches have a few of these 'ledgers', as they are sometimes called, but Wadhurst has by far the most in the country. One notable name recorded is that of Ann Benge, wife of William; he operated the nearby Gloucester furnace in the 1690s from which Sir Christopher Wren is reputed to have ordered the iron railings to encircle St Paul's Cathedral.

THE METHOD OF MANUFACTURE of these memorials was to make a bed of sand and press into it wooden blocks on which were carved all the relevant details; the imprinted bed was then filled with molten iron to a depth of some two inches and allowed to cool. The resultant slabs are extremely heavy. In order for the finished memorial to read correctly, the wooden die-blocks had to have details carved into them in reverse; on some Wadhurst memorials errors can be seen where the die letters have been carved the normal way round and so appear in reverse on the slab.

THE MAIN FRONT OF TICEHURST HOUSE, seen around 1920, much the same as it is today. This pioneering institution for the treatment, as opposed to the detention, of the mentally ill, dates back to the creation of an asylum in the 1760s by Samuel Newington (1739–1811). This burnt down in 1852 and the existing building immediately replaced it on the same site. In 1816 many traumatised Waterloo soldiers were employed in the therapy of laying out the gardens and walks for their hospital; these same walks survive today.

THE CROQUET LAWN AT TICEHURST HOUSE c. 1868. The vine-covered building was called The Museum, though what was on display is not known. As well as croquet, the extensive grounds also contained courts for tennis (grass and hard), badminton, a small golf course, and a cricket ground. Ticehurst House staff fielded two strong XIs up to the Second World War. Another much-enjoyed sport was bicycle polo.

THE LAST MEMBERS OF THE NEWINGTON FAMILY to administer Ticehurst House were (left) Dr Herbert F. Hayes-Newington and (below) his cousin, Dr A.S.L. Newington (1846–1914). The hospital passed from family ownership after the death of the former in 1917, aged 70. Dr A.S.L. Newington's house, Woodlands, built in 1882 on the edge of the estate, is today called Spindlewood, enjoying a new life as an attractive hotel and restaurant. In the 1920s a brochure described it as 'very comfortable accommodation for six ladies'.

THE GENERAL MEDICAL PRACTICE of Herbert's father, Charles (who lived at Highlands), covered many of the remoter parts of the parish. An anecdote he was fond of recounting was how, when on his rounds, he would meet smugglers moving through Bedgebury Woods in the evenings and they would say 'Good-night, doctor, Good-night, doctor' all down the line as he passed them.

THE GENTLEMAN'S DINING ROOM AT TICEHURST HOUSE, pictured around 1920. As is evident, great comfort was available to patients and there was a Concert Room where an orchestra performed every week during afternoon tea. Leading theatrical companies also visited regularly with their productions. Another distinctive amenity was a beautiful chapel. It formed part of the 1852 building and was renovated in 1891 by local craftsmen with multi-coloured walls ornamented with dado and frieze with, behind the communion table, a mosaic reredos set in carved oak. Regrettably, the chapel, a monument to the local community's caring instinct, did not survive large-scale alterations in the 1950s.

WADHURST SCHOOL, 1888/9. Masters: F.W. Larcombe and A. Rigg. Back row, left to right: W. Bassett, S. Ansell, T. Linkstead, ? Baldwin, ? Oliver, W.J. Piper, P. Tompsett. Second row: J. Bassett, ? Tidy, H. Watts, G. Watts, F. Piper, S. Smith, ? White. Third row: S. Wallis, J. Payne, N. Tompsett, A. Newington, W. Newington, E. Boyes. Fourth row: ? Tidy, H. Linkstead, C. Ashby, J. Skinner, S. Smith, M. Watts. Front row: F. Skinner, W. Watts, W. Wallis, C. Bassett. The original school was at Pell Hill, today Pell Bungalows, until the National School was built in 1854.

EDWARD CURRIE, 1805–89. From being a judge in India, he retired to live at Pickforde, Ticehurst, in 1864. He was village Sunday School superintendent and Day School manager from 1874 until his death. His son, Edward, was Dean of Battle from 1882 to 1920.

CAMPBELL NEWINGTON, 1851–1929. A notable Ticehurst philanthropist, and eminent Sussex public figure. As well as donating the Institute to Ticehurst, he was also a parish councillor and a JP at the old Hurst Green Court. From his home at Oakover he ran a farm of pedigree Sussex cattle and Southdown sheep.

THE SPACIOUS ARCHITECTURE OF TICEHURST INSTITUTE was by Sir Aston Webb, better known for his Victoria & Albert Museum, Admiralty Arch, Dartmouth Royal Naval College, and the frontage of Buckingham Palace. Donated to the village for 'lectures, concerts, village entertainments, classes and large meetings' by Campbell Newington, it was opened on 10 January 1900 and continues in its original purpose to the present day.

QUARRYING LOCAL STONE FOR TICEHURST INSTITUTE. Other materials used included Bath stone, York stone, and Oregon pine for the roof timbers. Depicted are clerk of works, Mr Gubb (centre), with Frank Ollive on the winch (far left) and Richard Balcombe in the apron (far right). The latter (1850–1934) restored much of the church and, when young, would climb the church spire to put the flag up before a flagpole existed.

H.M.S. PINAFORE.
TICEHURST

AN EARLY 1906 PRODUCTION at the new Ticehurst Institute. The cast are: Back row, left to right: Percy Field, Mr Reed, W. Cubitt, Mrs Woodroffe, Mr Nicholls, Revd Harvard, Mr Turnbull, Miss E. Moran, Mr Mabbutt, Frank Ford, Tom Field, Mr Martin, R.C. Morris. Middle row: Miss F. Vincent, Mrs Vincent, Mrs Hands, Mrs P. Field, Miss N. Field, Mrs Startin, Miss Wren, Miss E. Moren, Mrs Mason, Miss D. Allen, Miss L. Hardy, Mrs W.J. Field. Front row: Mr Hatcher, Mr Malpass, Mr Ames, Mrs Waight, Mr Waight, Miss L. Walter, Sgt J. Tinto, W. Mitten, Mr Hatcher jun.

PUPILS OF MISS MORRIS'S SINGEHURST SCHOOL, Ticehurst, around 1902. Back row, left to right: Renie Parker, Beatrice Waterhouse, Stella Maynard, Nicholas Daunt, Frank Dann, Harry Gillham, Connie Fleming, Louise Startin. Second row: Lily Daunt, Edie Waterhouse, Sissie Gillham, Lily Waterhouse, Alice Murrell, Evelyn Ford. Third row: Sissie Fleming, Bessie Gillham, Dorothy Colley, May Coppard, Marion Temple, Gertie Morris, Mabel Startin. Front row: Nora Murrell, Ethel King, Linda Gillham, Evelyn Williams, Reginald Field. According to Julia O'Dell, the Singehurst school dated from at least 1831, being described as a 'National and Sunday schoolroome'; it appears, however, not to have been where the farm of the same name is today, but on Singehurst owned land 'abutting the churchyard'.

MR F.W. LARCOMBE AND FAMILY, around 1920. Between them the Larcombes taught some four generations of Wadhurst children. 'F.W.' started in 1876, retiring in 1921; Mrs Larcombe taught up to 1920, when daughter Marjorie (centre) took over until 1952, while Gladys (left) retired in 1957 after thirty-nine years at Wadhurst School. The remaining daughter is Winnie.

THE OLD ETCHINGHAM SCHOOL class of c. 1920. The photograph owner is Mrs Mewett, pictured centre rear; other identities are not recalled. At this time the school taught some 70 children, the attendance having steadily declined from an all-time high of 150 in 1903. Not until the late 1950s was the old Victorian building of about 1862 radically modernized. Before then one headmistress, Florence Payling, always wore a hat to teach because swallows nesting in the eaves tended to fly about in the classroom. They were eventually excluded by netting the window.

CANDLE LIGHTING COY., TICEHURST.
TELEPHONE No. 21XX06.   TELEGRAMS, CANDLES.
INCORPORATED FEB. 1912.   J.R. 293

ENTREPRENEURS OF THE CANDLE LIGHTING COMPANY, Ticehurst, in 1912. Left to right: D. Hawkins, A.E. Field, G. Squibb, W. Pattenden, W. Chantler. With ladders and a cart of candles they went the rounds in the roads and lanes of Ticehurst in 1912 when the gas standards supplied by the Ticehurst Street Lighting Committee failed 'due to lack of subscriptions and a balance on the wrong side'. A local reporter proclaimed, 'Inhabitants have found it necessary to provide themselves with lanterns and electric torches to enable them to move about the roads at night with any degree of safety, and this is 1912!' But, working from a capital of 1s. 8d., the company men were soon a popular sight, 'carrying out their labour of light and love to their fellow men.'

WADHURST SCHOOLGIRLS MAYPOLE DANCING in Cheesman & Newington's field around 1910. Far right is C.W. Ashby, the mistress in the centre is Hannah Watson. The field was known as the Sports Field from c. 1922, after the creation of the Hall and Field Trust.

ETCHINGHAM SCHOOLCHILDREN continue the maypole tradition in their churchyard on May Day 1965 forming an interesting mix of pagan and parochial.

THE TICEHURST UNION was the parish work-house situated at the Ticehurst end of Flimwell village. Depicted are the master, Mr Wilson, and the matron, his niece, Miss E.M.L. Smith. The Workhouse survived virtually intact from c.1835 until the 1970s, being then demolished to make room for houses.

THE TICEHURST UNION WORKHOUSE in around 1914 with, in the foreground, village policeman Constable Crouch. About this time Miss M.T. Hardcastle visited an inmate called Mr Buckland. He had been born in 1824 and both his father and grandfather had been smugglers. As a boy he recalled being put on the back of an old horse on top of two tubs of 'sperets', hidden in baskets, and he rode them home and nobody thought of asking him questions. His father, born in Battle in 1796, was 'in the last big fight at Bulverhythe,' his life being saved only by a Revenue man's bullet hitting the metal 'tasty bottle' he carried in his breast pocket.

SOME OF THE ADMINISTRATIVE LEADERS OF THE WORKHOUSE; not all are identifiable. Back row, extreme left: W.M. Balcombe, third from left, Newton Taylor. Front row: -?-, -?-, Charles Balcombe, Mr Wilson, Mr Clark. The date is about 1890, and the oldest might have recalled the Agricultural Riots of 1830 when a band of rioters descended on the workhouse and 'summoned the Master who, being unpopular, was very roughly handled.'

TICEHURST SCHOOL, c. 1916. Back row, left to right: C. Copper, V. Holdcroft, F. Crouch, P. Morris, F. Field, M. Pilbeam, N. Gardner, D. Nicholls, P. Venner, W. Pilbeam, B. Cogger. Middle row: L. Tarry, A. Spiller, J. Pooley, L. Crouch, P. Field, E. Debley, H. Field, M. Wood, C. Crouch, L. Cogger, A. Todman, M. Larcombe, H. Harmer. Front row: W. Cartrey, E. Bates, E. Thompson, M. Rogers, G. Nicholls, D. Hobbs, N. Spiller, W. Todman, P. Harmer, F. Pilbeam, A. Pilbeam, S. Hobbs, N. Hobbs, M. Morris, B. Bates, A. Copper, G. Copper, D. Cogger. The school itself dates from June 1846, when the building which forms the nucleus of today's complex was constructed.

TWO BURGLARS BEING APPREHENDED by Wadhurst PC David Gander (in plain clothes holding a bag) outside the Red Lion. They are being taken to Mark Cross Court in one of W. Gadd's motors. Standing centre right (shirt sleeves, hands behind) is W.H. Newington; behind him (hand to collar) N. Buchanan, the hairdresser. The date is 1908.

TIDEBROOK SCHOOL, WADHURST, around 1903. The Tidebrook Glee Class gave a concert about this date which resulted in complaints to the vicar about its content. But this contretemps paled into insignificance when, in August 1944, a flying bomb exploded nearby, wrecking the school. It had served Tidebrook for some eighty-five years, but was never rebuilt. Luckily everyone was in shelters and there were no casualties.

THE SERGEANTS of 'C' Company (Ticehurst) 1st Cinque Ports Rifle Volunteer Corps at camp, around 1875. The only identity known at present is that of Jacob Field (seated centre) who was Col.-Sgt. Orderly Room Clerk. The 'soldiers of fortune' scenario may possibly derive from the Cinque Ports Volunteers' pedigree which went directly back to the great volunteer movement of 1803 to counter the Napoleonic invasion threat. During that year Lord Sheffield raised his 'North Pevensey Legion', which included a Rifle Company recruited from Ticehurst and Rotherfield parishes. He described his venture in an official memo: 'This is the largest and wildest Division of the County. There is a bad breed of smugglers, poachers, foresters and farmers's servants, who in the case of invasion are more to be dreaded than the march of a French Army, and unless some irremovable protection is afforded, no respectable person would abstain from removing to London.'

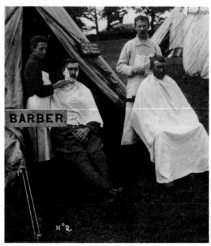

THE YOUNG CHARLIE BOCKING performing the lathering for his father at summer camp of the 5th bn. Royal Sussex Regiment at Moseham in 1912. The somewhat resigned recipients of the hairdresser's attention are George Cavey (left) and Harry Kemp.

RUDYARD KIPLING at the dedication of the Etchingham war memorial on 8 April 1920. The Nobel Literature prize winner lived nearby at Batemans, Burwash, from 1902 until his death in 1936. At this poignant ceremony his mind must have been filled with the memory of his son John's death with the Irish Guards at the battle of Loos, 1915.

COL.-SGT. INSTRUCTOR JOHN GEORGE TINTO, pictured around 1893, eldest son of John Tinto of Roberton, Lanarkshire. He served fifteen years with the Royal Sussex Regiment, including the Egyptian War in the 1880s, then ten years with the Cinque Ports Volunteers (Ticehurst). For some years the vicar's daughters, the Misses Eden, awarded a gold ring as the annual shooting prize for the Volunteers which the recipient could only keep permanently if he married within twelve months of winning it. Col.-Sgt. Tinto did this in 1907, winning the ring in the September competition, then in October marrying Caroline Blackah in Harrogate.

ONE OF THE SADDEST OF WARTIME PICTURES. The date is 20 August 1914, and the village working horses are being assembled outside the Bell in Ticehurst for transportation to the war. In most cases these horses were virtual family pets, having been born and bred on their homestead farms. They had enjoyed the most caring treatment and now were to be sent from a life of shelter and plenty to horrendous, lingering deaths in the quagmires of Flanders. The feelings of the men depicted saying farewell to their charges can only be imagined – and at this date it was still thought the war would be over in months.

HILL HOUSE during its time as a nursing home for wounded servicemen, some of whom are seen outside. Many Belgian refugees were sheltered at Wadhurst and Frant, some thirty-seven being cared for at Hill House by Mrs Boyd. By the end of 1919 over a thousand sick soldiers had passed through the old house, originally built in the 1740s by John Legas, Ironmaster. An iron threshold step, which may be original, is still in place at the road entrance.

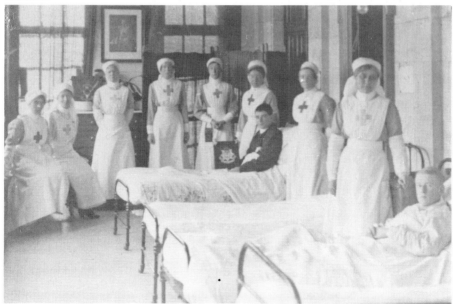

FIRST WORLD WAR VAD HOSPITAL at Shernfold Park, Frant, in 1915. Many of the patients were Belgian refugees, collected from the Channel ports by Frant residents in their private cars.

TICEHURST AIR RAID CONTINGENT, 1939–46. Standing, left to right: A. Livens (schoolmaster), J.F. Mansfield (retired PC), C. Atkins (farmer), F.A.R. Reeves (farmer), A. Hebditch (farmer), F. Goldsmith (carter), G. Wells (Wallcrouch postmaster), C. Croft (blacksmith). Seated: H. Waterhouse (grocer), B. Rich (gardener), Miss R. Collingridge (warden), Mrs Dengate (telephonist), V. Sinden (milkman). A *Sussex Express* publication, *The War in East Sussex* (1945), claims 'The first high explosive bombs on England in this war were five which fell at Ticehurst on May 22, 1940.' However, official files record that twenty-three incendiary and fourteen HE bombs were dropped near East Stour Farm, Chilham, at 4 a.m. on 10 May.

THE BACK OF BASSETT'S SHOP, FRANT, after a 1943 bombing raid. Mrs Alice Bassett (who was injured) later saw one of her sons become Parliamentary Private Secretary to Clement Attlee, with the result that the latter gentleman stayed above the shop on occasions during his premiership years between 1945 and 1951. An earlier bombing incident at Buttons Farm, Wadhurst, saw young Rose Eade win the George Medal for rescue bravery during a raid. She was 14 years old.

A NEWSPAPER ADVERTISEMENT from September 1944 depicting the original Doodlebug Alley. The alignment of the 'Alley' derived from the fixed firing sites across the Channel of the V1 Flying Bomb. Thus, most of those falling short of their target, or brought down by fighters before reaching London, landed in the area shown. According to official figures published in October 1944, seventy-six flying bombs exploded in the parishes covered in this book – Frant (16); Wadhurst (18); Ticehurst (31); Etchingham (11).

ACKNOWLEDGEMENTS

The compiler wishes to thank most sincerely the many people living in the area covered by this book who have contributed their generous help and expert knowledge. To those who have lent their valuable and unique photographs special thanks are rendered. These are:

the Trustees of the Bocking Collection, Wadhurst • the East Sussex Record Office at Lewes, for the Collingridge Collection • Mr & Mrs Meech of Wadhurst Councillor Pat Wright of Frant • the George at Frant • Mr & Mrs Polden of Little Bayham • Lady Killearn of Haremere Hall • L.A. Dengate, V. Catt, P. Lavallie, Mrs Mewett, and Mrs Springett, all of Etchingham • the *Courier* of Tunbridge Wells.

Others who are owed a debt of gratitude for their skilled assistance in the identification of specific photo features are:
The Imperial War Museum • National Motor Museum, Beaulieu RHM Foods Ltd • The Wealden Iron Research Group • Ticehurst Women's Institute • Bermans & Nathans Ltd • Chequers Garage, Goudhurst • and, not least, A.F. Drewe of Oakover, Ticehurst, for his knowledgeable help on the history of Ticehurst House, and also the Newington family genealogy.

With the help of the sources acknowledged above, the compiler has endeavoured to give as accurate a description as is possible of each photograph. Nevertheless, he remains well aware that, in some cases, deficiencies of identification persist. So, if any reader can supply the missing information, or indeed suggest corrections to that given, the compiler will be only too pleased to hear from them.